NASCAR Technology

Gail Blasser Riley
AR B.L.: 3.0
Points: 0.5   MG

The World of NASCAR

NASCAR Technology

by Gail Blasser Riley

Reading Consultant:
Barbara J. Fox
Reading Specialist
North Carolina State University

Content Consultant:
Betty L. Carlan
Research Librarian
International Motorsports Hall of Fame
Talladega, Alabama

Capstone
press.

Mankato, Minnesota

Blazers is published by Capstone Press,
151 Good Counsel Drive, P.O. Box 669, Mankato, Minnesota 56002.
www.capstonepress.com

Library of Congress Cataloging-in-Publication Data
Riley, Gail Blasser.
   NASCAR technology / by Gail Blasser Riley.
   p. cm. — (Blazers. The World of NASCAR)
   Includes bibliographical references and index
   ISBN-13: 978-1-4296-1289-0 (hardcover)
   ISBN-10: 1-4296-1289-4 (hardcover)
   1. NASCAR (Association) — Juvenile literature. 2. Stock car
racing — United States — Juvenile literature. I. Title. II. Series.
GV1029.9.S74R56 2008
796.72 — dc22   2007022734

Summary: Describes the technology currently used in NASCAR racing,
   including radios, safety devices, and the Car of Tomorrow.

Essential content terms are **bold** and are defined on the spread where they
first appear.

Editorial Credits
Mandy Robbins, editor; Bobbi J. Wyss, designer; Jo Miller, photo researcher

Photo Credits
AP Images/Chuck Burton, 12
Brian Cleary/www.bcpix.com, 5, 9
Corbis/Doug Collier, 8; The Sharpe Image/Sam Sharpe, cover, 13, 15, 17
Getty Images for NASCAR/Robert Meggers, 28; Rusty Jarrett, 11, 14, 22–23;
   Getty Images Inc./Doug Pensinger, 18, 25; Focus on Sports, 7
ZUMA Press/San Diego Union-Tribune/Charlie Neuman, 27; TSN/
   Harold Hinson, 21

1 2 3 4 5 6 13 12 11 10 09 08

Table of Contents

Running on Empty

"It's the only way we can win. I can make it!" driver Darrell Waltrip shouted. He was talking to his **crew chief** over the radio.

crew chief — the person in charge of a NASCAR pit crew

1989, Daytona 500

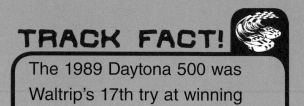

TRACK FACT!

The 1989 Daytona 500 was Waltrip's 17th try at winning that race.

Waltrip was low on fuel. His crew chief wanted him to stop for gas. But Waltrip was determined to win. He was sure he could make it to the finish line.

Waltrip's gas tank was almost empty as he neared the finish. His crew chief yelled over the radio, "Shake it, baby, shake it!" Waltrip steered back and forth to spill extra gas into the line.

It worked! Waltrip won the 1989 Daytona 500. Later that year, he became the highest paid driver in NASCAR history.

Waltrip crossing the finish line

Car Updates

NASCAR technology has come a long way since the sport began. Most improvements make cars safer. In 2007, NASCAR introduced the **Car of Tomorrow** (COT).

Car of Tomorrow — a new safer car style used in NASCAR's Sprint Cup series made to improve safety

Car of Tomorrow

11

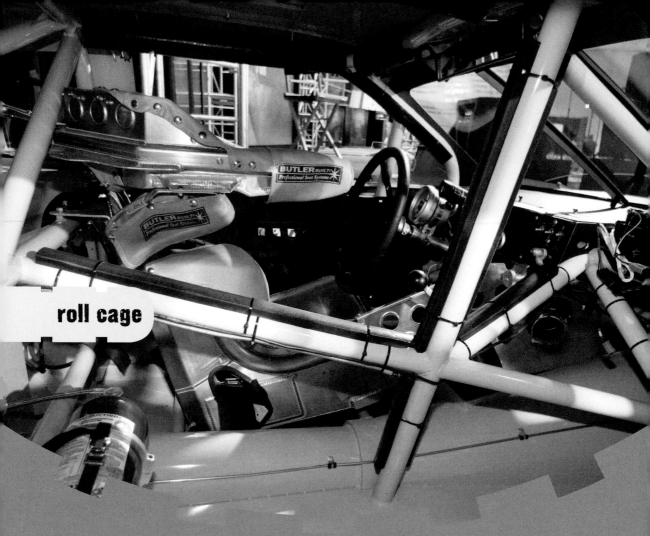

roll cage

TRACK FACT!

It took seven years for NASCAR officials to design the COT.

The COT has a larger **cockpit** and a stronger roll cage than earlier cars. A wall separates the engine from the driver's seat in case a fire starts. The COT also has a smaller, stronger gas tank.

cockpit — the area where the driver sits

Two other additions are the rear wing and front air dam. They make the cars easier to handle.

front air dam

rear wing

Each car carries a crash data recorder. It records what happens during crashes. The recordings help officials make future safety changes.

Apparel Upgrades

New technology keeps drivers safe and comfortable. Drivers wear *fire-resistant* clothing, full-face helmets, and a five-point seat belt.

fire-resistant — slow to catch fire

17

Dale Earnhardt Jr. wearing HANS system

The **Head and Neck Support** (HANS) system is another improvement. It supports a driver's head and neck in a crash.

Head and Neck Support — a system of straps that holds a driver's head in place in case of a wreck

New helmets keep drivers comfortable. A tube delivers water to a driver's helmet. The driver bites down to get a drink. Air-conditioned helmets keep drivers cool.

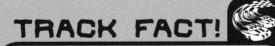

TRACK FACT!

Temperatures inside a race car can reach 115 degrees Fahrenheit (46 degrees Celsius).

drinking tube

Car of Tomorrow

roll cage

front air dam

racing tire

rear wing

racing tire

Extra Features

Drivers aren't the only people using new technology. Officials use headphones and radios to talk to workers in other areas.

Today's technology also draws
fans to the races. Fans at home and in
the stands can hear what drivers are
saying to their crews over the radio.

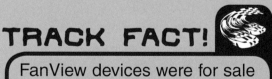

TRACK FACT!

FanView devices were for sale
or rent at all NASCAR tracks
in 2007.

Fans watch the action through
cameras worn by drivers. It's like sitting
in the driver's seat as the car whips
around the track.

2007, Martinsville Speedway

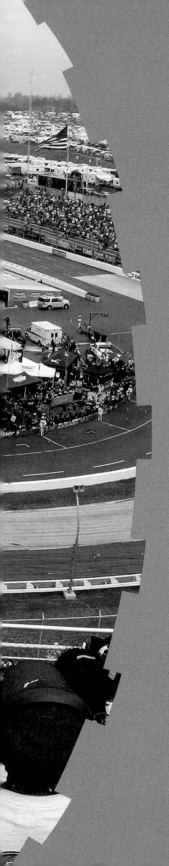

Since NASCAR began, technology has shaped the sport in many ways. Fans can only imagine what exciting changes will come next.

Glossary

Car of Tomorrow (KAR UV too-MAH-row) — a new car design used in NASCAR's Sprint Cup series made to improve safety

cockpit (KOK-pit) — the area in a stock car where the driver sits

crash data recorder (KRASH da-DUH ree-KORD-uhr) — a box inside a car that keeps track of information

crew chief (KROO CHEEF) — the person in charge of workers who service a race car

fire-resistant (FIRE ri-ZISS-tuhnt) — nearly impossible to burn

front air dam (FRUNT AIR DAM) — a body panel in the front of a car that cuts wind turbulence and creates a smoother ride

Head and Neck Support System (HED AND NEK sup-ORT sis-TEM) — a system of straps that holds a driver's head in place in case of a wreck

rear wing (REER WING) — a wing-shaped part attached to the back of a stock car that helps improve the car's handling

Read More

Gigliotti, Jim. *Fantastic Finishes: NASCAR's Great Races.* The World of NASCAR. Maple Plain, Minn.: Tradition Books, 2004.

Schaefer, Adam R. *The Daytona 500.* NASCAR Racing. Mankato, Minn.: Capstone Press, 2004.

Woods, Bob. *Live From the Racetrack: NASCAR on TV.* The World of NASCAR. Maple Plain, Minn.: Tradition Books, 2004.

Internet Sites

FactHound offers a safe, fun way to find Internet sites related to this book. All of the sites on FactHound have been researched by our staff.

Here's how:
1. Visit *www.facthound.com*
2. Choose your grade level.
3. Type in this book ID **1429612894** for age-appropriate sites. You may also browse subjects by clicking on letters, or by clicking on pictures and words.
4. Click on the **Fetch It** button.

FactHound will fetch the best sites for you!

Index